MW01245811

R̽ # JOHN 3:16

PATIENT: YOU

A
DAILY
DOSE

R_X # JOHN 3:16

PATIENT: YOU

A DAILY DOSE

HOLY BIBLE GENERIC FOR LIVING WORD
QTY: 40 DAYS
UNLIMITED REFILLS
AUTHORIZED BY DR. JEHOVA RAPHA

BENJAMON DEWITT YOUNG
NICHOL COTTON-HARDING
Xulon Press

Xulon Press
555 Winderley Pl, Suite 225
Maitland, FL 32751
407.339.4217
www.xulonpress.com

Paperback ISBN-13: 978-1-66288-577-8
Ebook ISBN-13: 978-1-66288-578-5

Acknowledgments

GOD
JESUS CHRIST
HOLY SPIRIT
Just want to also take a moment to thank a few individuals:
Our families, past, present, and future.
One of my students, Mr. Ashik Mia from Manikganj,
Bangladesh, assisted with bringing our vision to life on
the cover.

Dear Heavenly Father,

Thank you for being You. For loving us, caring for us, providing for us, and extending Your mercy and grace to us. We pray You continue to cover our family, relatives, friends, associates, co-workers, and even anyone who may consider us an enemy.

I pray that for the person reading this devotional, You meet them here and every time they pick up A Daily Dose, You open their eyes and bring clarity.

You are more than wonderful in all of Your ways! Thank you for giving us hope. Thank you for blessing me, the person reading this, and the generations to come with a generous portion of Your Holy Spirit. In Jesus's name.

Amen

DAILY DOSES

DAY 1

COME AS YOU ARE

"Come to me, all you who are weary and bur-
dened, and I will give you rest. Take my yoke
upon you and learn from me, for I am gentle
and humble in heart, and you will find rest
for your souls. For my yoke is easy and my
burden is light." - Matthew 11:28

Come as you are, as you were
As I want you to be
As a friend, as a friend
Take your time, hurry up
Choice is yours, don't be late
Take a rest as a friend
- Nirvana, "Come as You Are"

One of the things that I see quite often and hear quite
frequently regarding people wanting a relationship
with God is that they don't feel worthy, meaning somewhere
in their lives, a seed was planted that we have to be perfect

in order to have a relationship with God. I find the notion interesting. Imagine if we applied that notion to all of our relationships. What if we had to be perfect in order to know someone or to have a relationship with them? Shoot, we'd all be alone! We accept people, especially those we love, with everything that they bring, and we expect them to accept us in the same way.

God is not waiting for us to be perfect. God is waiting for us to be humble. God is not concerned about where we have been or what we have done. The omnipresent, omnipotent being that He is is only concerned about where we are and in particular, where we are with Him in Jesus Christ. So many folks are meandering through life looking for peace, searching for happiness, and hoping for love. It doesn't matter how much they obtain, how hard they work, or what they gain. Those things never fill the void. Inside, there is a thirst that can't quite be quenched; a deep desire or knowing for a greater purpose and at the same time, not quite knowing or understanding what the purpose is. That purpose is the calling. It's the Holy Spirit who wants to be reconnected with our Father. The problem is, there is a ton of world in between that relationship. The only thing that can remove the world is the Word!

In the earlier verse, Jesus said, "Take my yoke upon you and learn from me, for I am gentle and humble in heart." He is not asking us to be more than we can be. He is simply asking us to be more like Him. In order to do that, we must take the first step and come as we are.

Reflection: Will you take that step? What does that look like?

_____

_____

_____

_____

_____

_____

_____

_____

_____

_____

_____

_____

_____

_____

_____

DAY 2

WHAT DOES HE MEAN?

> Jesus answered, "I am the way and the truth
> and the life. No one comes to the Father
> except through me." - John 14:6 (NIV)

I woke up this morning with a mix of thoughts and scriptures scrambling through my mind. I was trying to make sense of everything, so I prayed, and a question hit me: What does Jesus mean to me?

My heart and mind rushed to all sorts of ideas and emotions, but scripture overpowered them all. Jesus said, I AM:

1) The Way
2) The Truth
3) The Life

So, I reasoned in my feeble, humanistic logic as to what this means exactly. The way (direction); the Truth (morality); the Life (purpose). When we accept Christ as our Lord and Savior, we automatically accept the means of a better and renewed life. The more that we pursue Him, the better our lives get. The less we pursue Him, well, it is what it is. Ignorance and disobedience come with a price.

*Reflection: Take a minute today and think of what Christ
means to you.*
*What does He mean to your life? How much of your daily life
is filled with His presence? Is your life a reflection of His presence or of His absence?*

_____

_____

_____

_____

_____

_____

_____

_____

_____

_____

_____

_____

DAY 3

THE POWER OF PRAYER

Therefore confess your sins to each other and
pray for each other so that you may be healed.
The prayer of a righteous person is powerful
and effective. - James 5:16 (NIV)

I notice in conversations with quite a few people that prayer is something either foreign or frightening to them. I often ask husbands and wives, "How often do you pray together?" I ask parents, "How often do you pray with your children?" Nine out of ten times, the answers are similar: "We don't," "I don't," "I can't recall," "Not hardly at all," or "Not nearly as much as I/we should."

My next question is always, "Why?"

Why do we fear sharing our greatest spiritual tool with others? And by "others," I mean the ones who we love the most! If we can't pray for and with the ones we love, then it is almost impossible to pray for and with those we don't know. Prayer is about faith, but prayer is also about humility. I can't think of anything greater than showing or teaching a child the reverence, respect, and humility of witnessing the person who gave them life on their knees, giving sincere thanks, praise, and appreciation to the Creator for blessing them with the opportunity to provide not only that life but the care of it.

We teach our children so many things, and this happens whether verbal or non-verbal, but the greatest tool that they will ever possess is their ability to communicate to God through Jesus Christ for themselves and for others. I see so many couples failing today, but it makes sense. They strive to obtain the world by working harder to achieve, but they neglect the power of prayer. We have to be active in putting God in every aspect of our lives because where there is no God through Jesus Christ, there is no love or truth. To be righteous only means to be filled with faith. If we trust God to fix or resolve an issue that is in accordance with His will, then we wait patiently for the issue to be resolved. When we understand that what we ask has been done, that is faith! Faith dictates many things! That is what makes it so powerful and effective!

Reflection: Who will you take the time to pray with today?

_____

_____

_____

_____

_____

_____

_____

_____

_____

_____

_____

_____

_____

_____

DAY 4

Talk to Me

If we confess our sins, he is faithful and just
and will forgive us our sins and purify us
from all unrighteousness. -1 John 1:9 (NIV)

One of the joys of friendship is communication. With a friend, we can laugh, cry, and talk about almost anything. In friendship, we are not afraid or apprehensive to be our authentic selves. I have learned that a key element of friendship is vulnerability. Friends listen, discern, and share, but the greater truth is that no one cares about how much a friend knows until they know how much a friend cares.

God, through Jesus Christ, is a faithful friend. The **ultimate** friend. He wants nothing more than to have an open, honest, and lasting relationship with you. God always thinks the best of us and wants the best for us. God is always pushing and encouraging us through Jesus Christ to be the very best versions of ourselves. Through His Word, we learn to talk to Him, and through His Word, we learn to listen to His counsel. His Word is the great separator between who we are, who we have become, who He is to us, and who we are trying to be in Him. He makes all things holy because He is holy. All we have to do is talk to Him with a sincere heart. Understanding that nothing that we do or have done can make Him love us any less. In fact, communication backed by humility makes Him love us even more.

Reflection: Is Jesus Christ your friend?
What do you talk about with Jesus? What do you want to talk about?

_____

_____

_____

_____

_____

_____

_____

_____

_____

_____

_____

_____

_____

_____

Ɍx

Lose the Wait

"Today, if you hear his voice, do not harden
your hearts as you did in the rebellion." -
Hebrews 3:15 (NIV)
- Luther Vandross, "Love Won't
Let Me Wait"

What is keeping you from God? The reply that I hear the most is "time." Time literally equates to life, as we are all on borrowed time; none of us can add to it, and none of us can take away from it, but the one thing that we can do, and do very well, I might add, is waste it.

In this fast-paced, busy world, time is our most precious asset. We know that every day we get older, and every day, our window of life gets smaller and smaller. The Bible says that many are called, but few are chosen (Matthew 22:14). How do we know that we are called or chosen? "Called" means that there is a yearning in your life that you can't describe. You know in your heart that you are meant for something better. "Chosen" is when you want a relationship with God, who is

Love, so you begin the process of building a relationship with Him through Jesus Christ.

When we don't answer our call, that is the same as hardening our hearts toward God. When that happens, the frustrations begin to kick in with one obstacle after another. The Bible says that once God begins a work, He will not stop until that work is complete. The Israelites hardened their hearts, and by doing so, had to wander in the wilderness for forty years instead of living lavishly with God in the land of milk and honey in the eleven days it would have originally taken (Ex. 16). In much the same way, our own disobedience, by procrastinating and waiting, is the greatest hindrance to our blessings.

The sooner we get right with God through His Word, the sooner our purpose is revealed and our lives take on new and unprecedented meaning. I want to encourage you to "lose the wait" today. Cut off anything that is keeping you from having a better relationship with God through His Word, which is Jesus Christ. Carrying the extra "wait" is like carrying a dead weight.

Reflection: What are you waiting for?

_____

_____

_____

_____

_____

_____

_____

_____

_____

_____

_____

_____

_____

_____

℞

DAY 6

FULL LOVE

> For whatever is in your heart determines
> what you say. - Matthew 12:34 (NLT)

The theory of relativity says that what goes up must come down. Well, the theory of spirituality works in much the same way because what is within must come out. We are all filled with something. Now the question is: What is that exactly?

Oftentimes, I find when it comes to believers (a.k.a. Christians), either there is an abundance of the Word in their hearts and lives or there is an absence, both, by observance and listening, are very visible and noticeable.

Whatever is stored in the heart will always find its way out, and this is true whether with hate or with love, compassion, or disdain. The heart is the centerpiece of our salvation. This is why the Bible teaches, "Above all else, guard your heart, for everything that you do flows from it" (Prov. 4:23 NIV), and the peace of God, which transcends all understanding, will guard your hearts and your minds in Christ Jesus.

The goal for all of us who consider ourselves Christians (a.k.a. followers of Jesus Christ) is to have our hearts filled to the brim and overflowing with love. First John 4:8 (NIV) says, "Whosoever does not love does not know God, because **God is love**."

In love, there is no room for selfishness or condemnation. There is only space for selflessness backed by truth, compassion, and understanding.

*Reflection: What are you **full** of today?*

_____

_____

_____

_____

_____

_____

_____

_____

_____

_____

_____

_____

_____

_____

MERCY, MERCY ME

For his anger lasts only a moment, but his
favor lasts a lifetime; weeping may stay for
the night, but rejoicing comes in the morning.
- Psalm 30:5 (NIV)

How many times in a day do we disappoint people we love—or even ourselves? Every day, we wake up to a new opportunity to make things right. We also have an opportunity to show mercy to others, as well, when they disappoint us. Repentance brings mercy, as there is nothing that God loves more than a humble and repentant heart.

Take a second today to take in a deep breath and tell the Lord how grateful you are for the life that you have been given. I want you to look beyond every problem, every flaw, every circumstance, and every situation in your life and just thank Him for life itself. Everything outside of that is irrelevant. Life through Jesus Christ gives you an opportunity to make the impossible possible; it gives you an opportunity to make all things in your life new. When we receive His mercy and we

give mercy to those around us, we are able to really understand grace. When we change our minds about the world, we
open up the power of the Spirit. The world will show us every
negative. The Spirit will show us how to overcome.

Reflection: What in your life are you asking God to show you mercy in? Who can you show that same mercy to?

_____

_____

_____

_____

_____

_____

_____

_____

_____

_____

_____

_____

_____

_____

_____

℞

PRESENT THE PRESENT

The fear of the Lord is the beginning of knowledge, but fools despise wisdom and instruction.
- Proverbs 1:7 (NIV)

Yesterday is history, tomorrow is a mystery,
and today is a gift that is why it is called the
present. - Unknown

In talking with both believers of Christ and non-believers, I
keep coming up with a common denominator in our conversations: the contrast between religion and relationship.
Religion is the thing that causes people to go to church. A
relationship is a thing that causes people to understand that
church is with them wherever they are. Religion doesn't take
much effort, whereas a relationship requires sacrifice.

I wonder how well our relationships would be with those
we love if we only spent a few hours a week with them. Could
we even call that love? Is that a relationship or is that religion?

Imagine if the people you love the most only gave you an hour per week. How would you feel about that relationship?

It is interesting to me that we treat this life like we have forever when we all are aware that we have an expiration date. All of our days are numbered. So, the question is, why don't we take salvation more seriously? Why do we waste the present dwelling on the past and forsake the potential of the future for the moment? The greatest gift that God gave to us is free will, and the greatest gift that we can give to God is ourselves. We can't say that we love, honor, respect, and obey Him if we give Him the bare minimum.

I have learned through Scripture that once God begins a work in someone, He will not stop until that work is complete. He will touch the things in our lives that we love the most to get our attention. Yes, that includes our children. Exodus 34:6-7 (NIV) says, "The Lord, the Lord, the compassionate and gracious God, slow to anger, abounding in love and faithfulness, maintaining love to thousands, and forgiving wickedness, rebellion, and sin. Yet He does not leave the guilty unpunished; he punishes the children and their children for the sin of the parents to the third and fourth generation." And Matthew 10:37 (NIV) says, "Anyone who loves their father or mother more than me is not worthy of me; anyone who loves their son or daughter more than me is not worthy of me."

As people, we tend to procrastinate, but in regard to spiritual matters, time is of the essence. Your presence is required in the present. If life is weighing you down, that is a clear indication that God is trying to prompt you to turn to Him wholeheartedly. He will keep turning up the heat until you get the point. The sooner you take the step toward Him, the sooner your life and the lives of those around you will improve. Present yourself to God, and He will present Himself to you.

Reflection: What new/additional steps can you take to help you seek Him?

_____

_____

_____

_____

_____

_____

_____

_____

_____

_____

_____

_____

_____

DAY 9

I, ME, US, WE

> Accept the one whose faith is weak, without quarreling over disputable matters. - Romans 14:1 (NIV)

> You, then, why do you judge your brother or sister? Or why do you treat them with contempt? For we will all stand before God's judgment seat. - Romans 14:-10 (NIV)

> Hurt people hurt people. Healed people heal people.
> - Unknown

Something we all forget more times than not is that we are all in this together. This is true whether we believe or doubt, have faith or lack thereof. Life automatically makes us universal. Where we are spiritually is where the divide begins.

One misconception of non-believers is that Christian's (a.k.a. people who believe in Jesus Christ) don't struggle or fail. People automatically associate Christ with the highest of standards; therefore, anyone who professes to follow His ways must be held to that same standard, which is perfection. We tend to not factor in the fact that we are all works in progress. We are Spirit-trapped in a dying and decaying body. Failure is inevitable. The goal is to be humble and repentant, to keep striving, to get better—because if we know better, then we are obligated to do better. We have to allow each other to grow spiritually or at least be courteous to one another's faults while trying to assist one another in being and doing better.

The truth is, we all struggle. We all have a natural way about us that wants us to rely solely on our emotions, feelings, opinions, ideas, and agendas. It's the soul side of who we are. The spiritual side of who we are sees beyond that. Its sole reliance is upon God and not the self.

Let us understand that we are all made in, from, out of, for, and to love. It is our common denominator, as God is Love. We are not here to judge one another. We are here to assist one another in love, that is, if assistance is requested. I may not be able to force my love on you, but I can wrap you in it. I can embrace you in a way with it that you don't feel condemned. How am I able to do this? The same way that Jesus did. He didn't force anyone to do anything. He just lived the life of love and truth that He was supposed to live. There were those who accepted it and those who rejected it, but in the end, He never wavered in who He was. He wasn't hurt, so He had no reason to hurt others. He is love, and that is exactly what we all have received.

Be encouraged to bless someone today. Allow God to speak to you about the needs of others. Wait for it, watch for it, then respond in kindness. The best way to be blessed is to always be a blessing. We are in this together.

Reflection: How will we work together?

_____

_____

_____

_____

_____

_____

_____

_____

_____

_____

_____

_____

_____

_____

DAY 10

GLOW IN THE DARK

For we live by faith, not by sight. - 2
Corinthians 5:7 (NIV)

This little light of mine. I'm gonna let it shine.
Let it shine. Let it shine. Let it shine. - "This
Little Light of Mine"

F aith dictates that we walk through this life blind; not necessarily knowing or understanding, but always hoping that God not only will but is guiding our course. Personally, I've had many times in this life where I didn't think that I had enough inside to go on. There were many times when I couldn't see a way and many times when I felt that I lacked the physical ability to take another step, but God always pushed me through the darkest times of my life. He taught me how to glow in the dark.

I've been seeing in the dark for quite a while. Thanks to His grace and endless mercy, I see the effect that it has had on my children and on people in general. I realize the importance of shining bright in the darkest of times and at the darkest of moments. I realize how valuable light is to others. When we dim, we dim others. When we glow, we illuminate others.

You may not believe this, but you are a miracle! You are a blessing! Within you lies the potential of greatness. A potential that cannot be stopped or altered! Your ability to love can far exceed that of anyone else's. Everywhere you are, with the Holy Spirit, everywhere you go, darkness has to flee in your presence because Jesus has so ordained it within us! And what's inside always has to find its way out! This flesh can't contain the Spirit! Darkness can't overcome the light!

Reflection: In what ways has God pushed you or is currently pushing you to be the light in your darkness?

_____

_____

_____

_____

_____

_____

_____

_____

_____

_____

_____

_____

_____

_____

MIRROR, MIRROR

As water reflects the face, one's life reflects
the heart. - Proverbs 27:19

The Bible summarizes when we accept Christ into our lives, we receive a renewed heart, a renewed mind, and a renewed spirit. Many people think that it's the mind that guides us, but it's not. It's the action or intent that steers the course of our lives. The heart of who we are has more control over us than any one part of our bodies.

What do you see when you look in the mirror? Are you proud of the totality of your work up to the present day, or do you have room for spiritual improvement? The truth is, the heart doesn't lie. Everything that is stored up in it finds a way out. Our job is to do the very best that we can to reflect the image of love. After all, that is the mirror of God.

Reflection: When you look at your life, what do you see? When others look at your life, what do you believe they see?

_____

_____

_____

_____

_____

_____

_____

_____

_____

_____

_____

_____

_____

_____

Shhhh, to Listen

The Lord said, "Go out and stand on the mountain in the presence of the Lord, for the Lord is about to pass by." Then a great and powerful wind tore the mountains apart and shattered the rocks before the Lord, but the Lord was not in the wind. After the wind, there was an earthquake, but the Lord was not in the earthquake. After the earthquake came a fire, but the Lord was not in the fire. And after the fire came a gentle whisper. When Elijah heard it, he pulled his cloak over his face and went out and stood at the mouth of the cave. Then a voice said to him, "What are you doing here, Elijah?" - 1 Kings 19:11

How many times in our lives have we pleaded for God to speak to us or give us a sign when in reality, we are surrounded by His reminders all day every day? We ask God for a sign but don't get the message because we are looking, listening, and waiting for answers in the flesh, and God speaks to us through the spirit. Oftentimes, what we want or desire is in contradiction to what He is telling us, so we wait and wait for the "big bang." We eagerly await for God to just scream at us; however, we must remember that when God speaks, He speaks in a gentle whisper. We should intently listen for that whisper so we do not miss what was said. We are too busy listening to the external noise or the voices inside of our own heads instead of waiting for God's will to prevail.

We live in a world that is buzzing with nonstop sounds. Even in our quietest of moments, we are hard-pressed to have total silence. Background noise like phone notifications, alarms, or something going on in the distance like the TV. God's Word filters all of these things out because God's Word is noise canceling. In fact, it's noise counseling, but we have to be still and quiet in our hearts to each able to hear and to be able to listen.

Reflection: What are you listening for? What's your background noise?

_____

_____

_____

_____

_____

_____

_____

_____

_____

_____

_____

_____

_____

_____

_____

_____

_____

_____

℞

HELLo from Us, HELLO from Him

You, Lord, are forgiving and good, abounding
in love to all who call to you. Hear my prayer,
Lord; listen to my cry for mercy. When I am in
distress, I call to you, because you answer me.
- Psalms 86:5-7 (NIV)

When the phone rings or chimes, we look at the caller ID, and the response depends on whether or not we feel like being bothered. Do we feel like talking to the person who calls? Maybe it's a timing issue, but in any sense, we can be too busy in our hearts and our minds to answer, so we let the call go to voicemail. That's just us as people. We get a notification, and we can easily swipe it off our phones. On the contrary, we can call a friend, and they can do the same, no matter how important the person is to us or we are to them.

God, on the other hand, answers every call, and He hears every prayer. He is always attentive to where we are in Him. He is always available. Anytime, anywhere, He is there. His response may not align with our desires, but He always provides the proper counsel and the proper course. We just have to be able to listen beyond our emotions and hear with the Spirit that we have been so graciously given rather than with our intentions.

Reflection: Can you remember a time that no one picked up when you needed them? How about when you cried out to God. How was He there?

_____

_____

_____

_____

_____

_____

_____

_____

_____

_____

_____

_____

_____

_____

R⃰
X

DAY 14

EASY AS 1, 2, 3

For everyone who asks receives; the one who
seeks finds; and to the one who knocks, the
door will be opened. - Matthew 7:8

Life is really simple, but we insist on making
it complicated.
- Confucius

In the Bible, Proverbs 3:34 says, "God opposes the proud but
rejoices with the humble," which basically translates into
the fact that pride is our greatest enemy, especially in regard
to spirituality and a greater relationship with God.

Pride will keep us from asking, and pride will keep us
from receiving. Pride will keep us from searching, and pride
will keep us from finding. Pride will keep us from knocking;
therefore, doors will always be closed to us. Our pride is very
misleading.

Humility, on the other hand, asks and receives. It helps
and is helped. It seeks, and it finds, but most importantly, it is

found. Humility doesn't run or hide. It's accessible! Humility understands that it needs grace, mercy, and forgiveness more than anyone, and under this truth, it has no problem in giving it in abundance to all freely. It's as easy as 1, 2, 3!

Reflection: Is pride making your life difficult? What steps can you take to practice humility?

_____

_____

_____

_____

_____

_____

_____

_____

_____

_____

_____

_____

_____

_____

DAY 15

LAST RESORT FIRST

> But seek first his kingdom and his righteous-
> ness, and all these things will be given to you
> as well. - Matthew 6:33 (NIV)

Trust in The Lord with all your heart and lean not on your own understanding. - Proverbs 3:5 (NIV)

Life happens to all of us. "This comes up" and "that comes up" at every twist and turn. We search for a means, a solution, or a remedy, only to find ourselves perplexed and bewildered. We sit in awe of the situation, hoping for an answer to present itself, and in our hopelessness, we think to ourselves, *I have done all that I know to do!*

In our flesh, this is the response; however, when we are in our flesh, we tend to completely overlook and neglect our spirit. The reality is that we should have started with God first! Before we "tried this" and before we "tried that," we should have taken our requests and petitions to God. When we get in a habit of placing God at the forefront of our lives and decision-making process, then we will get the results and favor that we desire.

*Reflection: How can you make seeking God your first resort
instead of your last?*

_____

_____

_____

_____

_____

_____

_____

_____

_____

_____

_____

_____

_____

_____

DAY 16

ALL THAT AND THEN SOME I AM

> God said to Moses, "I am who I am. This is
> what you are to say to the Israelites: 'I am has
> sent me to you.'" - Exodus 3:14 (NIV)

Look in the mirror—what do you see? Close your eyes and imagine yourself from head to toe. What do you see? You know yourself well, right? We all know ourselves, and in the knowing, we are many things. We carry many titles and abbreviations, but not a single one of us on Earth—past, present, or future—can describe ourselves in just two words: "I AM."

We are neither omnipresent nor omnipotent! Even at our absolute best, we can't compete, compare, understand, comprehend, or rationalize God at His bare minimum. I love the scripture above for many reasons, but the simplicity of it gives me chills. Tell the people, "I Am who I Am!" That is powerful! To be everywhere and nowhere at once, being the Alpha and the Omega! Constantly creating and flowing beyond our wildest imaginations and through it all, caring about such insignificant things like you and me. He knows the number of every strand of hair on our heads!

Reflection: What and who do you see when you look in the mirror?

_____

_____

_____

_____

_____

_____

_____

_____

_____

_____

_____

_____

_____

_____

61

THE LIGHT SHINES BRIGHTEST

You, Lord, keep my lamp burning; my God turns my darkness into light. - Psalm 18:28 (NIV)

The eye is the lamp of the body. If your eyes are healthy, your whole body will be full of light. - Matthew 6:22 (NIV)

Your eye is the lamp of your body. When your eyes are healthy, your whole body also is full of light. But when they are unhealthy, your body also is full of darkness. See to it, then, that the light within you is not darkness. Therefore, if your whole body is full of light, and no part of it dark, it will be just as full of light as when a lamp shines its light on you. - Luke 11:34

I'm up so early in the morning that I don't like turning on the lights because of the brightness, especially in my closet.

So, I keep a solar lamp that provides just the right amount of light to see what I need to see and do what I need to do.

I notice that if I set the lamp on the ground, only the things that are at its level are illuminated, but if I place the lamp on my top shelf, it provides light for the entire closet.

Much is the same way for our lives. It is said that the eyes are the windows to the soul. You can look into someone's eyes and see what type of mood they are in. You can find happiness, joy, excitement, and light, or you can find sorrow, misery, anxiety, and darkness, just to name a few.

As I stated earlier, when I place my lamp at the highest point in my closet, it brings light to the entire closet. At its lowest point, it doesn't produce much light. Keep in mind, there is no change in the amount of power that it has. The power is in the elevation.

We have to be mindful of the light within us, and we have to be careful of the darkness that is in us as well. The key is to always keep the light elevated. Depression makes one lower their head. Confidence causes one to raise theirs. We should always be confident in the Lord. After all, His is the light that shines brightest. Keep shining, my friends!

Reflection: How are you keeping your light from going dim?

_____

_____

_____

_____

_____

_____

_____

_____

_____

_____

_____

_____

_____

_____

THE COST OF CONVENIENCE

> "I have the right to do anything," you say—
> but not everything is beneficial. "I have the
> right to do anything"—but not everything
> is constructive. - 1 Corinthians 10:23 (NIV)

Everything that we do or say and don't do or say has a cost associated with it, just as for every action there is a reaction. The Bible uses simple terms for this principle, and it's probably one of the oldest in the book—it's called the law of reaping and sowing.

Freedom, choice, free will; God has given us so many options. He allows us to make choices and to decide our fates. In a world where we can be and do almost anything, we have to be reminded that not everything is worth being and not everything is worth doing; not everything is beneficial.

There are pros and cons to everything in this life because life is about give and take. Sowing and reaping is one of the oldest biblical principles, and it permeates through every civilization and time. The type of seed we plant is the type of harvest we will yield. Every choice and every decision is weighed; everything that is done, and even everything said. In fact, it also works in reverse. The things that we don't do and say have repercussions.

Life is about discernment—knowing better and doing better. It's about always striving to be the best person that we can be for not only ourselves but for others. It's about leaving everything and, hopefully, everyone better than we found them. When asked what the two greatest commandments were, Jesus replied, "Love God with all of your heart, soul, mind, and strength; and love your neighbor as you love yourself" (Mark 12:30-31, paraphrased). By honoring these two, we honor all ten.

Reflection: What are you sowing? What is it costing you?

_____

_____

_____

_____

_____

_____

_____

_____

_____

_____

_____

_____

_____

_____

_____

LEAN INTO IT

Trust in the Lord with all your heart and lean not on your own understanding. - Proverbs 3:5 (NIV)

When I was in the Army, I was stationed with an infantry unit in Fort Ord, California. Every Friday morning, we would do a fifteen-mile road march, then a twenty-five-mile road march once per month. Our very last road march was ninety-six! That's a lot of walking! There were times that we would encounter extremely steep hills, and in some cases, the hills were so steep that they were vertical. We were taught to lean into the hill as we progressed forward. It made the climb easier and took the stress off of our bodies. In many ways, to me, as a young soldier, leaning into the hill didn't make much sense, partly because I was stubborn and just wanted to do things my own way, but in the end, leaning was the right way. Leaning in made it a tad bit intense.

How many times in our lives do we go against the grain of God's instruction because we want to do the opposite of what is asked of us? We want to question and make sense of a situation or circumstance. We think that we know how best to overcome an obstacle or situation, only to find that our way was much more complicated.

Today, I want to encourage you to lean into the challenge of not trying to understand what God is asking you to be doing in your life but accepting whatever He advises through His Word. You trust that whatever it may be, it is going to be far greater than anything you could have ever anticipated.

Victory does not come in the beginning. Victory does not come in the middle. Victory only happens in the end when the work is done! When we finally made it to the top of that hill, there was always a deep feeling of satisfaction and gratification. We could see things from the top that we never imagined while at the bottom. The hard work made sense. By leaning in and shifting the weight, the effort paid off.

Reflection: What can you do to begin to lean into God?

_____

_____

_____

_____

_____

_____

_____

_____

_____

_____

_____

_____

_____

_____

DAY 20

LIVING ON A PRAYER

> Do not be anxious about anything, but in
> every situation, by prayer and petition, with
> thanksgiving, present your requests to God.
> - Philippians 4:6 (NIV)

Person of faith: Why are you stressed? Why are you anxious? Why are you worried? Are you living off of what you see, or are you living off of what you believe? Are you living on a prayer? Are you trusting in the promise?

You see, the thing about our God, through Jesus Christ, is that He does not lie. He is faithful to the very end! God promised us that He would never leave us nor forsake us. He sent His Son to carry us through all of our troubles, trials, and tribulations! Our job is to be humble, obedient, and repentant, and our duty is to pray without ceasing. A spiritual life without prayer is not a spiritual life at all. We should be living on a prayer at all times.

A DAILY DOSE

Reflection: What have you been consumed with? Have you been living on a prayer?

_____

_____

_____

_____

_____

_____

_____

_____

_____

_____

_____

_____

_____

_____

CANNED HEAT

Do not be quickly provoked in your
spirit, for anger resides in the lap of fools.
- Ecclesiastes 7:9 (NIV)

Anger—we all have it, we all deal with it, and we have all dealt with it. It is, without a doubt, the most destructive emotion that we carry. It is a neighbor of hate but makes hate look pale in comparison because without anger, hate is just a bark without a bite.

I used to be a very angry person. And the truth is, I didn't even realize it. It was a subtle anger, smoldering in the ashes waiting to consume. As I grew spiritually, I learned that it was a generational curse, as my mother was a very angry person. I had inherited her trait as she had inherited the trait from her father.

The Bible taught me that it is not a sin to be angry, but it is what we do with our anger—out of speech or action—that is the sin. The Book of James says that "we should be quick to listen, slow to speak, and slow to become angry" (Jms. 1:19

NIV). In other words, God gave us two ears and one mouth for a reason—so that we could listen twice as much as we speak. We can't help one another if we can't hear one another. We can't heal one another if we can't help one another. The goal is to open the heart and can the "heat." It's foolish to live in anger because the one who lives in anger will also die in and by anger. Anger, if left unbridled, is a consuming fire and will destroy any and everything in its path. It will leave a scorched mouth and a bitter heart; not a single one of us can be bitter and better at the same time.

Let go and let God!

Reflection: Are you angry in any way? Who feels the heat from that anger?
Let go. Now, breathe ...

_____

_____

_____

_____

_____

_____

_____

_____

_____

_____

_____

_____

_____

_____

DAY 22

HURTS TO HEAL

> And our hope for you is firm, because we
> know that just as you share in our sufferings,
> so also you share in our comfort.
> - 2 Corinthians 1:7 (NIV)

In this world we live in, people are afraid to be vulnerable. Everyone has a wall up. Everyone is guarded. Not many want to air or share their struggles for fear of ridicule or abandonment. The truth is, every last one of us struggles with something. Some have taken the power of the struggle and used it to their advantage, to the advantage of God, because any and everything that is withheld consumes while things that are set free are controlled and offer deliverance.

As spiritual people, we should own our hurt because in our hurt, there is help for ourselves and for others. It is impossible to do the will and work of God while walled up like Jericho! No, the walls of our lives must come down. The pain must be set free so that the testimony can be revealed! How many people are waiting for you to release your hurts so that they can release theirs? How many people are waiting for you to take a spiritual step forward so that they can take a spiritual step forward? In order to fully receive comfort, we must first be comforting. Everything that hurt us on the inside has the power and the ability to heal someone somewhere if we release it.

Reflection: What hurt are you holding on to? Release it to God. Begin to embrace the healing in your life and watch it help heal others.

_____

_____

_____

_____

_____

_____

_____

_____

_____

_____

_____

_____

_____

_____

THE COMPANY *YOU* KEEP

> Do not be misled: "Bad company corrupts
> good character." Come back to your senses
> as you ought, and stop sinning; for there are
> some who are ignorant of God—I say this to
> your shame. - 1 Corinthians 15:33-34 (NIV)

God provides so many lessons for us in everyday life. Some are blatantly obvious, and some are very subtle. We used to say, "One bad apple will ruin a bunch," and how true it is. So, we knew to either remove the bad apple or remove the bunch immediately because it would be just a matter of time before freshness was compromised.

The very same philosophy or logic applies today. It applies in our everyday lives and with every relationship that we encounter, whether intimate, personal, professional, or even spiritual. You see, there are five warnings, or parts, to the above scripture:

1. Do not be misled; be the spiritual leader and not the worldly follower.
2. Bad company corrupts good character; notice that it does not say that it "might corrupt" or "maybe it'll corrupt." No, it's a definite, a done deal, in just a matter of time. (This is something also to ponder when allowing our children to sleepover at a "friend's" house.)
3. Come back to your senses; in other words, do what you know is right to do.
4. Stop sinning!
5. Do not be ignorant of God; do not confuse the love of God for the love of the world.

The wrong person or people will inevitably make us the wrong person. Trying to fit in and get along with a worldly process only leads to destruction. There are some people out there who carry a different spirit, and that spirit's sole purpose is to seek and destroy. It wants to seek out God's people and manipulate them to either second guess the Spirit of God or abandon it altogether. Those spirits would rather see us as we were, in and of the world, as opposed to how we are trying to be in and of Christ!

*Reflection: Inevitably, the company that we keep also keeps us. Are **you** in bad company?*

_____

_____

_____

_____

_____

_____

_____

_____

_____

_____

_____

_____

_____

_____

_____

_____

_____

WHY IS IT?

You, dear children, are from God and have overcome them, because the one who is in you is greater than the one who is in the world. They are from the world and therefore speak from the viewpoint of the world, and the world listens to them. We are from God, and whoever knows God listens to us; but whoever is not from God does not listen to us. This is how we recognize the Spirit of truth and the spirit of falsehood. -1 John 4:4

Why is it that we can say and send memes and jokes, songs and videos, of all sorts of debatable and disputable things without second-guessing, but when it comes to sending scriptures or prayer or praying with someone or giving a spiritual insight, we debate internally? We question if we should or shouldn't and prolong sending it.

Why is it so easy to respond or do things of the world but so hard, complex, and difficult to follow the instructions of the Word? Why do we struggle with it? Why is it that we can watch movie after movie and listen to song after song, singing every lyric as if we wrote it ourselves, yet when we pick up our Bible to read just a few words, we are instantly sleepy, and our minds can hardly contain the words? How much Scripture do you remember?

The answers to all of these questions are simple: We are programmed by the world from birth. The first thing that happens when we accept Christ is that we receive a renewed heart, a renewed mind, and a renewed spirit, but within these gifts, we also have to put in work. Just as the body needs physical activity and good nutrition to function properly, so does the spirit. The Bible says that we are in the world but not of the world (see John 17:11-15). It's okay to sing, dance, laugh, and enjoy life. The key is to have more of the Word in our lives than the world. We have to dilute the world within us with the Word.

Reflection: What are you doing with the world? What are you doing with the Word?

_____

_____

_____

_____

_____

_____

_____

_____

_____

_____

_____

_____

_____

_____

_____

Rx

DAY 25

WATCH YOUR MOUTH

The tongue has the power of life and death, and those who love it will eat its fruit. - Proverbs 18:21 (NIV)

The tongue also is a fire, a world of evil among the parts of the body. It corrupts the whole body, sets the whole course of one's life on fire, and is itself set on fire by hell. With the tongue we praise our Lord and Father, and with it we curse human beings, who have been made in God's likeness. Out of the same mouth come praise and cursing. My brothers and sisters, this should not be. - James 3:6, 9-10 (NIV)

When God created the world, He spoke everything into existence. God said, "and it was so," (several times in Genesis chapter 1). and being that there was nothing in space to stop His omnipotent, omnipresent voice,

His voice is still carrying and creating to this very day. That is power! Think of all of the things we accomplish with our mouths and words daily. In the same breath that we build, we also can destroy. The versatility of our tongues. Our words hold weight. This tongue we have can tell someone, **"I love you" (bringing life), but can also tell someone, "I hate you" (bringing death).**

How many times have I spoke things into existence? In my youth, I said that I was going to get drunk, get laid, and get into a fight the coming weekend, and everything that I spoke came into existence, followed by even greater trouble. Our words always precede our actions. Our words are a reflection of our innermost being, and from the overflow of the heart, the mouth speaks. I know people who speak all day every day about how bad they feel, and guess what? They never feel good. They never feel like doing much. I know people who talk negatively about their lives and self-image, and yup, their lives never change, and their view of themselves never improves. I know people who constantly speak of their poverty and then wonder why their financial situation never changes. I know people who think and speak constantly of the negatives of their past; therefore, their past has taken charge of not only their present but also their future.

Sadly, not only do we allow our own thoughts and words to destroy us, but we allow the thoughts and words of others to do the same. I'm here to tell you today that the only opinion that matters about you is God's. Everything else is just speculation or a distorted image. Only God truly knows you!

If we want spiritual improvement in our lives, we should be mindful of what we bring to our lips. Watch your mouth! Sure, things may not be great at the moment, but if we profess in faith that God is renewing, rebuilding, restoring, recreating, reinvigorating, changing, building, blessing, establishing, administering, fixing, and completing every aspect of our lives and then hold on to the faith that He is faithful, then those things are going to come to pass in Jesus's name!

*Reflection: What are **you speaking** into existence?*

_____

_____

_____

_____

_____

_____

_____

_____

_____

_____

_____

_____

_____

_____

WHAT'S IN A WORD?

Taste and see that the Lord is good; blessed
is the one who takes refuge in him. - Psalm
34:8 (NIV)

What's in a word? We use them all day every day. Some are thoughtful, some are thought-provoking, and some are reckless. Words. They carry so much weight and power. With words, we lift up and we destroy. Kingdoms are built and wars are waged by words. In the flesh, we speak flesh, and in the spirit, we speak spirit. Our words bring forth life. What's in a word? I question mine from time to time, but when I read and study God's Word, I have zero doubts.

As believers of Jesus Christ, what's in God's Word is what's inside of us. The power activates when we take the time and make the time for it in our lives. It renews and transforms our minds, taking us further from our former way of life while creating a new life of truth and love for us.

Reflection: What word is in you?

_____

_____

_____

_____

_____

_____

_____

_____

_____

_____

_____

_____

_____

DAY 27

THE SPIRIT YOU CHOOSE

> He replied, "You are talking like a foolish woman. Shall we accept good from God, and not trouble?" In all this, Job did not sin in what he said. - Job 2:10 (NIV)

What separates Job from many of us was his willingness to accept whatever trial or tribulation came his way. Job chose to see God in every aspect of his life, regardless of how bad things got. He lost everything that this world would consider important, but he maintained trust in God.

I hear a lot of people talking about happiness. I know many people who are searching for it daily—people whose happiness is contingent upon them feeling good. If life is favorable, they are full of joy, but if life is unfavorable, they are full of grief and misery. Did you know that happiness is a spirit, just as unhappiness is a spirit, and depression is a spirit? The reality is that these are spirits of emotion! Our happiness is not contingent upon what we have or who we have in our lives. Genuine happiness can only be obtained by appreciation, gratitude, and gratefulness. Like Job, it's the knowing that no matter the circumstance or situation, God is in absolute and total control! There is peace in that understanding.

Now, we can choose to understand and accept this simple spiritual fact, or we can choose to follow the frail misgivings of our emotions, which are like the waves of the sea, blown and tossed by the wind. The beauty of free will is that it's a choice. The ugliness of free will is when we choose to go against the grain of God's will and purpose for our lives.

Reflection: What spirit do you choose?

_____

_____

_____

_____

_____

_____

_____

_____

_____

_____

_____

_____

_____

_____

_____

WHATEVER

> Finally, brothers and sisters, whatever is true, whatever is noble, whatever is right, whatever is pure, whatever is lovely, whatever is admirable—if anything is excellent or praiseworthy—think about such things. Whatever you have learned or received or heard from me, or seen in me—put it into practice. And the God of peace will be with you. - Philippians 4:8

Sometimes it's easy to throw our hands in the air and say, "Whatever!"

Sometimes it's easy to let our mouths spew words that promote death rather than life. Whatever.

Sometimes it's easy to take a nonchalant attitude about important matters. Whatever.

Sometimes it's easier to quit than it is to keep going. Whatever!

What if we switch it up like the apostle Paul?

Paul wrote around 85 percent of the New Testament. He was committed, and he was invested. Keep in mind, most of his writing was done while he was either imprisoned or in situations that were unfavorable to his being, but he took a "whatever" attitude and pressed forward spiritually.

> **Whatever a person thinks they become.**
> Proverbs 23:7 (KJV) states, "As he thinketh
> in his heart, so is he."

Our thoughts have so much power over our being. An unwell thought will produce an unwell being. The apostle Paul encourages us here to elevate our thoughts, to keep our minds set and focused on whatever is good, to do whatever we can and not allow our minds to wander to places that will lead our hearts in a negative direction. The truth is, where our thoughts go, we are sure to follow.

Reflection: What is your "whatever" thought?

_____

_____

_____

_____

_____

_____

_____

_____

_____

_____

_____

_____

_____

_____

You May Be

> How, then, can they call on the one they have
> not believed in? And how can they believe
> in the one of whom they have not heard?
> And how can they hear without someone
> preaching to them? And how can anyone
> preach unless they are sent? As it is written:
> "How beautiful are the feet of those who bring
> good news!" - Romans 10: 14-15 (NIV)

A question that I ponder quite often is, "How can I help someone spiritually if I can't hear them?" If my mind is filled with preconceived notions and animosity, there is no way that my heart will be willing to listen. In fact, it's the opposite; it becomes dismissive.

Every day, I realize that people have been lied to spiritually, and through those lies, there are misconceptions and misunderstandings about God. I remember a time I was one of these people. Then I read the Word for myself, and now I study to show myself approved. The fact is, religion is destroying lives. This is why I am set on teaching about "relationship."

I spoke with someone the other day who is a non-believer, and they practice a completely different type of faith/religion. I'd like to say that this is uncommon, but it's not. I accept people for who they are and just try to share what I've learned. I realize that there are many things that can divide us as a people, but one thing unites us all. That one thing is love! The power of it! The ability to want to receive it or the ability to want to give it. God is Love. So, everyone wants God! We just don't know or agree on how to get to Him. I prayed with this person the other day, and after the prayer, their reply was, "No one has ever prayed with me before." And now, we start to understand the problem.

How are they going to learn if there is no one to teach them? We have to be willing students in order to be able teachers. I can guarantee that there are many people in your life who are disconnected spiritually, and you may just ignore them. Other people or situations may look too challenging. I want to encourage you today to pray for those people. Pray that God will make a way to use you in their lives spiritually. While you are praying, think of this simple thing:

You may be **the only person** praying for that person.
You may be **the only person** concerned for their soul and their salvation.

Reflection: Who are you "the only person" for?

_____

_____

_____

_____

_____

_____

_____

_____

_____

_____

_____

_____

_____

_____

_____

DAY 30

MISS COMMUNICATION

I call on you, my God, for you will answer
me; turn your ear to me and hear my prayer.
- Psalm 17:6 (NIV)

The eyes of the Lord are on the righteous,
and his ears are attentive to their cry. - Psalm
34:15 (NIV)

The righteous cry out, and the Lord hears
them; he delivers them from all their troubles.
- Psalm 34:17 (NIV)

Talk with God, no breath is lost. Walk with God, no
strength is lost. Wait for God, no time is lost. Trust in
God, you will never be lost. - Kristiyano Tayo We talk all day,
but who is really listening? Name a person that truly understands
your heart and knows the innermost person of your being. I'll wait.

The God that we serve through Jesus Christ, He loves to
listen. Not only does He love to listen, but He lives to reply.

The Bible said that when God spoke to Elijah, He spoke in a gentle whisper (1 Kgs. 19:12). I believe that many times in our lives, we miss what God is saying because:

1. We are too busy talking to listen (we tend to listen to respond rather than listen to listen).
2. We are waiting on a "big bang" rather than a gentle whisper.
3. With so much noise happening around us, and with not enough of the Word in our lives, we fail to filter out the sense from the nonsense, so we miss the communication.
4. And then there are those who simply don't talk to God at all or only speak when they are in trouble or in need. God misses genuine communication from us. Speaking to God should be as thoughtless and as organic as breathing. We don't count our breaths. We simply breathe. Talk to God as you would the love of your life. Be encouraged to share the depth and breadth of your heart. There is no time like the present. You don't have to miss Him, and He does not have to miss you.

*Reflection: Are you missing communication with your
Heavenly Father? What will you do to fix that?*

_____

_____

_____

_____

_____

_____

_____

_____

_____

_____

_____

_____

_____

_____

_____

_____

DAY 31

HABITAT FOR HUMANITY

By wisdom a house is built, through understanding it is established; through knowledge
its rooms are filled with rare and beautiful
treasures. - Proverbs 24:3

Lord, I love the house where you live, the
place where your glory dwells. - Psalm
26:8 (NIV)

How we start our day sets the tone and tempo for the
entire day, but the night before sets the stage for the
morning. How we end is how we begin, and how we begin is
how we end. Spiritually speaking, we are, or should be, constantly building habitats for humanity.

I like to keep things simple. In the morning, when our
consciousness kicks in, our first thoughts should be, *Thank
you, Lord, for this new day. Thank you for Your favor and
blessing.* Our heart and mind should be filled with prayer,

thanks, and supplication, as like a good builder, we are laying the foundation for the day.

As the day progresses, we are giving thanks, praise, and prayer and asking for mercy, guidance, and forgiveness. Being repentant is like laying down brick after brick of faith, hope, and love.

By the end of our day, before we close our eyes, we are thanking God through Jesus Christ for blessing our day, teaching us, helping us to be better today than we were yesterday, and being a vessel, giving Him all of the glory, honor, and praise, which is like placing the roof on our spiritual home with the blessing of His covering over us.

House completed!

Tomorrow, God willing, we will rise and start the process all over again. A house down, and many more houses left to build. Be encouraged to not make your spiritual life more complicated than it needs to be. Prayer, thanks, humility, and faith is all that is required. Those are your supplies. Your lumber, mortar, hammer, and nails. Everything that you need to spiritually succeed resides inside of you. A heart that is used to build is also a heart that is used to help and heal.

Reflection: Are you building your spiritual house?

_____

_____

_____

_____

_____

_____

_____

_____

_____

_____

_____

_____

_____

_____

BIBLE

> Remember the days of old; consider the generations long past. Ask your father and he will tell you, your elders, and they will explain to you. - Deuteronomy 32:7 (NIV)

I believe we can all say with truth that history has a way of repeating itself. What has been done will inevitably be done again. The reason is that the heart of mankind for centuries hasn't changed much. Our basic needs and desires have been the same since our existence. The only thing that has changed is our means by which to acquire and the amount of which we can gain—or lose.

Remember the days of old. Consider the generations of long ago. I find myself thinking of my ancestors quite a bit. Their struggles, trials and tribulations, and faith. I think of what they had to endure for me to be here today. It always brings me back to Scripture. The Bible is a compilation of history and lessons. We look at people who had favor with God and worked to emulate their example. We also look to people who opposed God and worked to avoid their calamity. We learn from those who were humble and from those who were disobedient. We understand that in order to receive the blessings of God, humility is our best course of action, as no one wants to carry the curses for disobedience.

Everything that we spiritually need to succeed has been provided for us. It is laid out in manuscript form, page by page, step by step, and scripture by scripture. The Bible teaches that my people perish for lack of knowledge. The pursuit of it is never-ending. The goal is to gain, practice, and share as much of it as we can with future generations so that they can, in turn, share it with the next generation(s). This is the mission before leaving this earth, with the knowledge so many mistakes can be avoided.

Reflection: If you haven't picked up the Bible, I encourage you to just read a scripture or two a day. You can use the scriptures in this devotional to start. Meditating on the Word daily will bring you revelation in such a way that will transform your relationship with Christ. The Word is alive. Write down the scriptures that stand out to you, and start there. You got this!

_____

_____

_____

_____

_____

_____

_____

_____

_____

_____

_____

_____

_____

DAY 33

SAME AS IT EVER WAS

What has been will be again, what has been done will be done again; there is nothing new under the sun. Is there anything of which one can say, "Look! This is something new"? It was here already, long ago; it was here before our time. No one remembers the former generations, and even those yet to come will not be remembered by those who follow them. - Ecclesiastes 1:9

Jesus Christ is the same yesterday and today and forever. - Hebrews 13:8 (NIV)

With so much going on in the world, it may seem that we are experiencing something new. It may feel as though things are changing or that the times are different. Truth is, it's not. The fact is that our knowledge is limited by the present, but the present is not limited to our knowledge. Every single thing that has been done today has been done before in a previous generation; the only exception to the rule is the time and technology.

The heart of man has always been the same. The heart of God has always been the same. And the heart of God's people has always been the same. Those that are for Him have always been for Him, and those who are against Him have always been against Him. It literally is the same as it always was. We are just getting to a place in our physical and spiritual lives where we are all going to meet Him sooner rather than later.

Reflection: Can you take a moment and point out the things that feel new? That are really the same? How are you learning from the past?

_____

_____

_____

_____

_____

_____

_____

_____

_____

_____

_____

_____

_____

Rx

I, GOD, You

Love is patient, love is kind. It does not envy, it does not boast, it is not proud. It does not dishonor others, it is not self-seeking, it is not easily angered, it keeps no record of wrongs. It always protects, always trusts, always hopes, always perseveres. Love never fails. - 1 Corinthians 13:4-5, 7-8 (NIV)

Dear friends, let us love one another, for love comes from God. Everyone who loves has been born of God and knows God. Whoever does not love does not know God, because God is love. - 1 John 4:7-8 (NIV)

What is love? Every day, I see that it means different things to different people. Love is based on our wants, needs, or desires. It's based on how we feel at any given moment. Love has fueled our societies and civilizations since the beginning of time. Every generation has been on a quest to unlock its secrets and embrace its touch. I ask again: What is love to you?

When I got saved in 2008, I learned that love is not a "what," an "it," a feeling, or an emotion, but rather, it's an all-encompassing who! Love is I Am, and I Am is Love.

Love is not selfish by any means, but we as people are. Think we aren't? We would kill a flower just for its beauty! I would like for you to really think about the Bible's definition of love.

Now go back, read it again, but this time, replace the word "love" with "God."

Ah, epiphany!

Everyone wants God, but the problem is, people have been taught wrong by a society of bad habits and selfishness. Selfishness is the cornerstone of capitalism. It creates the love of making money, and that becomes a god to some. An idol, in a sense.

When I see problems in relationships, I automatically know that one of two things is missing: love or truth. We can't have sound relationships without these two key things.

Love is God, and **Truth** is Jesus Christ. You can't have the Father without having the Son; no one can have love without truth.

Reflection: When you replace the word "love" with "God,"
what does that say to you about love?

_____

_____

_____

_____

_____

_____

_____

_____

_____

_____

_____

_____

_____

_____

DAY 35

WHAT YOU WON'T DO

> Dear friends, let us love one another, for
> love comes from God. Everyone who loves
> has been born of God and knows God.
> Whoever does not love does not know God,
> because God is love. God is love. Whoever
> lives in love lives in God, and God in them.
> - 1 John 4:7

I was listening to some classic soul this morning, and a song
by Bobby Caldwell called "What You Won't Do For Love"
came through the shuffle. It's definitely a classic, but as I was
listening, it really made me ponder the question in a spiritual
sense. Love (God) makes the world go round! Whether this
side of the globe or that side of the globe, this culture or that
culture, this language or that language, our common denominator is love.

We rise, we shine, and we fall for love. We do all that we
can for it. It's not the fact that we enjoy working that causes
us to work; it's the fact that there are people in our lives who

need us, that drive and motivate us to support them. We love them, and we want to see them thrive. We love ourselves, so we feed and shelter ourselves.

Love is so profound, so universal. So, the question is: If you are not in it for love, then what are you in it for? We do so much for human love. In fact, we will go above and beyond and out of our way for it, but the question that lingers the most in my heart and mind is: What won't you do for God?

Reflection: How far are we willing to go for God? How much are willing to give? How much are we willing to sacrifice for the love that matters the most?

_____

_____

_____

_____

_____

_____

_____

_____

_____

_____

_____

_____

_____

_____

℞

DAY 36

LOVE AND HAPPINESS

Take delight in the Lord, and he will give you
the desires of your heart. - Psalm 37:4 (NIV)

Whoever does not love does not know God,
because God is Love. - 1 John 4:8 (NIV)

What does it mean to be "happy"? I hear this word all
of the time, as so many are in pursuit of it. The real
question is: Are you, as a Christian, happy? What does happiness mean to you?

But before you answer these questions, I want you to
think about this first ...

How many times is the word "happy" mentioned in the
Bible? I'll help—zero! The Bible says that we can be content
(Philippians 4:11). We can be thankful. We can be filled with
the Holy Spirit, which, in my mind and opinion, supersedes
all feeling and emotion, but "happiness" is an option created
by the user, not the Creator. In other words, we are searching
for something that we already possess. The problem is we

overlook what we have because we focus too much on what we desire. However, if we desire God, then we desire love—selfless, agape love; the kind that you can't buy, that which transcends all levels of understanding because God is Love and love should be the epitome of happiness!

It amazes me how love permeates every aspect of our lives, yet the true meaning and importance of it often go overlooked or unnoticed. We mask love behind emotions, feelings, and needs.

Reflection: So, I ask again, are you, as a Christian, happy? If not, are you truly pursuing love with all of your heart, soul, mind, and strength?

_____

_____

_____

_____

_____

_____

_____

_____

_____

_____

_____

_____

_____

_____

_____

R
X

DAY 37

THE REaDy SEE

The Lord will fight for you; you need only to
be still." Then the Lord said to Moses, "Why
are you crying out to me? Tell the Israelites
to move on. Raise your staff and stretch out
your hand over the Red Sea to divide the
water so that the Israelites can go through the
sea on dry ground. I will harden the hearts
of the Egyptians so that they will go in after
them. And I will gain glory through Pharaoh
and all his army, through his chariots and his
horsemen. - Exodus 14:14-17 (NIV)

Much like us today, the Israelites were in a very precar-
ious position. They had just left Egypt, the only land
in which they had known, and were headed into unknown ter-
ritory while being led by a man named Moses, who, in many
ways, they were uncertain of. They come to the foot of the
Red Sea. There is a mountain to the left of them and a mountain to the right of them. Pharoah and his vast army were

rapidly approaching from the rear, insistent on destroying them. Talk about uncertainty and terror!

How many times in your life have you been surrounded by issues that you thought were going to destroy you?

How many times have you been boxed in by the stresses of the world?

Everything that the Israelites went through, they went through for a reason. It was not by chance; it was all by design. I say again—we are much like them! God was leading them to the Promised Land! A land of milk and honey. God is doing the very same thing with us who believe and are faithful! The only thing keeping us from reaching that destination or prolonging our journey is our lack of obedience and or faith!

God will always provide the opportunity, but we have to be ready for the moment!

How many times have we talked ourselves out of a promotion for fear of rejection or because we didn't think that we were qualified?

How many times have we given up one breath short of our breakthrough?

How many times have we cried when we should have been rejoicing?

Y'all aren't hearing me! But the REaDy See!

Reflection: Take a moment and think about situations when you were surrounded and facing a Red Sea. Will you be REaDy to see through it the next time?

_____

_____

_____

_____

_____

_____

_____

_____

_____

_____

_____

_____

_____

_____

_____

DAY 38

Angels Among Us

> Do not forget to show hospitality to strangers, for by so doing some people have shown hospitality to angels without knowing it. - Hebrews 13:2 (NIV)

I'm not sure what you know, and I am not sure what you believe about teachings regarding angels and demons being among us. The Bible is very sound about how these entities move around us daily. The more we digest the Word of God, the more visible they become. The more cognizant of their presence in and around us we become.

I used to work part-time in the evenings at a local Walmart. Every day, a homeless man would sit on a bench by the side entrance. He carried a backpack, a guitar, and a device for picking up litter. He never asked for a thing. Every day I passed him to enter the store, I asked him if he needed anything, if he was okay, or how he was doing. He always smiled and said, "I'm fine." I offered him food and money, but he always declined.

What I found interesting about this man was that as people approached the door, whether coming or going, he always got up from the bench and opened the door for them. Once again, he never asked for a thing. He just did. He was always polite and was always courteous.

Even now, I'll see him walking around the parking lot picking up litter and occasionally walking through the aisles shopping for a few grocery items. I am convinced that this man is an angel. "Angel" in Greek and Hebrew means "messenger." The message that this man sends to me is very clear. It is that life is not about what you have or don't have. It's not about how you look or what you wear. It's about being gracious in whatever circumstance you are in. It's about doing good without the notion of expectation because good is simply the right thing to do. I get the message loud and clear, and I pray that you have received it as well.

Reflection: Do you see the angels among us? What do they look like to you?

_____

_____

_____

_____

_____

_____

_____

_____

_____

_____

_____

_____

_____

_____

R
X

Ready for the World

"Do you now believe?" Jesus replied. - John 16:31 (NIV)

"I have told you these things, so that in me you may have peace. In this world you will have trouble. But take heart! I have overcome the world." - John 16:33 (NIV).

-or-

"I've told you all this so that trusting me, you will be unshakable and assured, deeply at peace. In this godless world you will continue to experience difficulties. But take heart! I've conquered the world." - John 16:33 (MSG)

D o you believe? This is a question that Yeshua/Jesus asks us daily. Well, do you? Many of us can say that we do with our mouths, but do we really, with our hearts?

When our personal world is upside down, do we look at the *matter*, or do we look at the *fact*? When the health report isn't in our favor, when the relationship is falling apart before our eyes, when the addiction has a grip on us, when disconnect notice after disconnect appears in the mail and you're afraid to answer the phone because creditors keep calling and your expenses exceed your income, when you feel like there is nothing left to give and you don't understand why you are living ... do you believe?

Jesus is the Provider of peace. Satan is the god of this world. We can see clearly that this world is full of problems. It is full of hurt and suffering, death and decay; however, it is also full of life. We who believe are the light of the world. Christ lives in us, and His light shines in the darkest of places. Every opportunity to be righteous is an **opportunity**. We are ready for the world, and faith dictates that the world is ready for us. We just have to believe that through Him, we can change it!

Reflection: Do you believe?

_____

_____

_____

_____

_____

_____

_____

_____

_____

_____

_____

_____

_____

_____

℞

DAY 40

BELIEVE IN THE
BLESSING OF YOU

For I know the plans I have for you," declares the Lord, "plans to prosper you and not to harm you, plans to give you hope and a future. Then you will call on me and come and pray to me, and I will listen to you. You will seek me and find me when you seek me with all your heart. I will be found by you," declares the Lord. - Jeremiah 29:11-14 (NIV)

The will of God is not for us to fail. In fact, it is for us to succeed. How do I know this? Because Scripture tells me so. This is not a prosperity gospel; this is a biblical fact. The first thing that Jesus preached was "Repent, for the kingdom of heaven is at hand" (Matt. 3:2 NKJV). True, He was speaking of His presence, but He was also speaking about a good life. So many people are waiting to die to see Heaven, yet they are denying a heavenly life while here on Earth by worrying or stressing or second-guessing.

151

I go back to the words, "I know the plans I have for you," and then I think about the blessing that followed. Everything about us has been designed with a divine and supernatural purpose. We carry both the spirit of victory and the spirit of defeat within us. How we feed or fuel either one on any given day dictates our future. It decides whether we win or lose.

Jesus told the people that their faith would make them well. He is telling and has told us this very same thing today.

> **Faith is the substance of things hoped**
> **for and the evidence of things not seen.**
> **- Hebrews 11:1 (NIV)**

What we believe dictates what we obtain and how we obtain it. If we believe in God through Jesus Christ, then no door is locked, and every seemingly impossible way in our lives has now been made possible.

With each breath, we draw nearer to our destiny every day. We as believers are closer to Christ than we know.

Reflection: We believe in the blessing of you. The question is, do you believe and embrace the blessing of YOU?

_____

_____

_____

_____

_____

_____

_____

_____

_____

_____

_____

_____

_____

_____

_____

Printed in the USA
CPSIA information can be obtained
at www.ICGtesting.com
CBHW021452240924
14863CB00052B/845